D1280917

1

EVERY WOMAN DOES NOT DESIRE A HUSBAND OR TO BE MARRIED

$\mathcal{M}$any of us did not grow up with fathers in the household, exposure to positive male role models, or in a household where love was a positive experience. I am a mixture of all of these. I am the fourth surviving child of parents that married while my mother was pregnant with me. My mother loved everything about my dad, the good, the bad, and the ugly. She loved him unconditionally—until she did not. They remained married and separated because she was Catholic and did not intend to pay for a divorce. My father was not the marrying type; however, he came from a family like my mother's and understood responsibility. My grandfather was the marrying type, and if my paternal grandmother had had options, I do not

1

believe she was the marrying type. My maternal grandmother loved love and was the marrying type for all the right reasons. Unfortunately, her choices were not always the best, but she had good taste in men, and I learned a lot about love from her, my mom, and my grandfather, who I affectionately referred to as Grand Pop.

My parents officially separated when I was 10 years old. I loved my dad and could not understand why my mother could not or would not just do whatever he needed her to do so he would not leave. After a brief reconciliation and being old enough to see the domestic abuse, I finally understood the dark side of love.

I adored my father and enjoyed the perks of being his Baby Girl. As the youngest of three girls, I was pretty protected by my brothers. With the love of a strong family, I did not go looking for love in the wrong places, and I was secure with myself. As a family with money insecurity, what we lacked in things, Momma and her village made up in love and laughter. I truly had no idea I was poor until I was older and on my own, figuring out that Momma had raised six children on a salary that I was making as a single woman with no responsibility.

I never really thought of marriage, was not a

believer in fairy tales, and had never seen happily ever after. I mean really, there were no Black men with horses in my neighborhood, and I had not seen many men rescuing women.

The stories of Black love to which I was exposed were more common-law, men with two families (pre-Internet), or the second wives club. The handful of successful marriages were incredible for me to watch. I was grateful that the women found many questions funny and the men found my curiosity charming. Miss Irene and Mr. Jimmy were a joy and would often take me fishing. I would watch their interactions and smile: She was a Southerner, and her mannerisms were not like anything I had seen before. Their disagreements were brief and often ended with her giving him a look, never raising her voice, and usually winning the fight. **She would tell me that a lady has to learn how to fight but never embarrass her husband in public. This lesson would come back to me early in my marriage.**

I had many opportunities to observe my Granny Florence with her last husband Carlos, who we called Fat Daddy during the good years, the fighting years, and through the divorce. While it wasn't pretty, they had a daughter, my Aunt Lou, and figured out how to make it work. It helped that she had a strong village of women warriors and was financially secure after the divorce. Her village included educated, beautiful women who worked and had a "piece of the pie" stashed away and husbands that supported them as well. A few were girlfriends to Fat Daddy's friends who Granny tolerated. However, the words behind their backs were ugly. She did not like entertaining the girlfriends of his married friends, and she once asked one of the girlfriends if she entertained Fat Daddy's girlfriends at her house. **Witnessing that fight when he got home taught me another lesson that would be major in my marriage.** It was also the first time I thought that I would probably not ever get married; I was not sure I was marriage material or if I had any desire to be someone's wife. Why not be a girlfriend who could leave anytime you wanted and not be too vested in the relationship? Her sister circle also taught me the importance of the village, securing your own money, and that security is not love.

That summer, my young self decided I would date a lot. I would not wait on my Prince Charming and would prepare for a childless life with a few boyfriends. I shared my knowledge with my granny, and she popped me in the mouth for being grown.

Education was the single most important aspect of growing up in our house. After my parents separated, I had the privilege of going to Catholic school. I attended from 5th grade through 10th grade. I spent my teenage years living in a Black neighborhood and attending a white school. With only a handful of Black male students, I went my entire stay there without being asked out once on a date by a classmate. We did a lot of group hangouts, flirting, and partying, but I am not one to change myself for the comfort of someone else. If you cannot come to my front door and pick me up, we are not going out. I was sure my brothers were not having some white person show up in our hood to take their little sister out. Besides, I had enough homework to keep me busy for eight years, and I had a very active social life. By my first year of high school, I had had enough boy friends in title that boyfriends were not a priority. Besides the drama of my siblings and their relationship issues, I was once again committing to a life without a husband or children. At the rate I was going, I began to speak my plan into existence. I was sounding selfish, but I had my siblings and a growing number of nieces and nephews.

In my junior year of high school, I transferred to the public school and began to focus my attention on the next steps. Get out of school, go into the Air Force, and travel the world on the dime of the US Government. Many friends, male and female, went into different branches of the military and were doing well. I just needed to get through high school.

Being the new girl in any school is never easy; however, it was the first time I had been in school with my family and friends, and I was having the time of my life. A few weeks into school, I began to flirt with Mr. Green Eyes, a guy that sat next to the table I shared with my brother, cousin, and the neighborhood fellas. Mr. Green Eyes had a girl-friend, but it did not stop his friends from encouraging him to flirt back. I had to let him know I did not date other people's boyfriends. I had gone on a few dates, and life was good, but I was still good with not falling in love. I would occasionally see my flirt, and in the last week of summer, he asked for my phone number and proceeded to lose it three times before he finally called.

On the first Friday of our senior year and after my first Varsity football game as a cheerleader, our first date was a disaster. He saw me "flirting" with another classmate, who happened to be one of my best friends, and he left. The whole incident left me laughing. We ended up going out the next night.

Within a few months, he had asked me to be exclusive and not date anyone else. By Christmas, I was in love.

I was not ready. I did like being part of a couple. However, love was already complicated, and I had many questions. The early lesson on love was that sex was not love, and I was not about to let love or young sex ruin my plans.

Hearing my mom and some of my friends talk about the security of a man, a new word entered my vocabulary: security. What did that mean? What did it look like? My mom had been in a long-term relationship at this time, and it could be very volatile at times. I was not looking for security, but I sure liked being in love.

Unlike my granny's friends, my mom's friends were mostly single, separated, or divorced women. My mom was parochial school and business school educated and stood out. However, like her mother, she loved love and always bet on love.

Some ups and downs, breakups and make-ups and life lessons learned, Mr. Green Eyes and I married 10 years after graduating as high school sweethearts...

QUESTIONS OF DISCUSSION:

Do you desire the marriage or the wedding?

_____

_____

_____

_____

Do you enjoy being around him 24/7? Is he a friend? Do you enjoy just hanging out?

_____

_____

_____

_____

Do you share the same values?

_____

_____

_____

_____

2

BEFORE YOU SAY, I DO... TALK ABOUT CHILDREN

 y greatest achievement in life was birthing two beautiful healthy children. Fear kept me on birth control because I had no intention of being a single mother, and my granny had told me, "Don't be like your Momma; only have enough kids that you can carry out the door when you leave." I know that is harsh, but I am grateful for that advice.

As we enjoyed our first year married, our summer vacation, my husband literally said one day, "Next year we are gonna try for a baby and you're gonna have to quit smoking."

I laughed and told him, "As long as you know if you leave you're taking them with you." I went off the pill, and two months later, I was pregnant.

9

All my girlfriends told me it would be months for my cycle to regulate and probably take a year or two to get pregnant. I was PREGNANT in two months. I loved every single day of my pregnancy, and my husband was in heaven. Both families were excited, and our friends were so happy for us. Things were coming together. Why was I scared to death?

I'd spent a lot of time babysitting as a teenager and made a lot of money. To me, children were about making money, not spending money. I had five nieces and nephews before leaving high school. I have many cousins, and they have many children. I had my fill of children and never felt maternal; I was good to be the loving, cool auntie. I never craved children, barely played with dolls, and no matter how many times my granny told me I would make a good mother, I was okay without children. I had decided I would be okay without them. I was certain this was a non-negotiable for me and moved through life as a woman that didn't want children.

During my single years when Mr. Green Eyes and I were on hiatus, I barely dated men with children. The few I did date hardly ever resulted in a third date. I tired of listening to men blame women for all their woes and why they could not be part of their children's lives. How they blamed the mother of their children for needing money to feed, clothe, and pay for daycare for their children. It never made sense how they could not or chose not to fight for their children. This really hit home the day the doctor placed my son in my arms; my whole world changed.

How could a man walk away from his child? How could a man put himself before his child? How could a man not go to work every day to provide for his child? Why are we having babies for boyfriends that do not see us as wife material? Not only was I the marrying type; I was willing to give my husband a baby because he wanted one, because he asked for one, and because we loved each other and our child was an extension of us.

Mr. Green Eyes was just the type of father he promised me he would be loving, attentive, and involved. Our love was flourishing, and we were happy. He thought we should add another; however, I was not ready.

My career was on a new trajectory, and everything was falling into place. How would two children affect us?

We welcomed our baby girl four and a half years after her brother with the full support of our village that went out of their way to say yes more than they said no.

Your support system is more valuable than your family, and if by chance you have family in your support system, count your blessings. We have a strong village that has supported our marriage, excellent godparents for our children, and mothers that offered great advice and babysitting services in a pinch. We also had excellent childcare with Shyrel "Miss Bep" and her extraordinary family. They quickly became our family. Since we did not live in the same city as our blood family, they became my sisters, aunties, and cousins. She was such a trusting soul to me, offering advice in a loving and caring way. All these years later, a random stop at her house leaves me feeling loved.

Children are gifts from God. I feel forever blessed that God bestowed our two upon us, but I do not regret waiting until I was married to my soul mate before bringing them into my life. I felt like an old woman having babies, but my "security" relieved my concerns, and the partnership of my marriage afforded me balance. I knew this was not how most families lived, and I was grateful to be in love, married, and a mother. Life was good.

We found a good balance; however, there were

many years when I was at the office way past dinner hour and came home to a house of chaos and attitude, grabbing dinner on the way home and staying up to do homework. Traditional parenting roles were not working for us and became the issue of some of our early arguments.

With sports beginning to consume our life, there was very little downtime for us. This was new territory. We had always made time for date night, and we had not shifted to prioritizing ourselves. In my mind, the children were the priority. Once Mr. Green Eyes purchased his motorcycle, my jealousy and envy monster showed up. How could he have private time and I was working just as many hours at home as I was at the office? I began to blame him for things that were not his fault; how dare he not do more? This period of our marriage was entering a new phase, and I was not balancing it well.

One night we were actually arguing about who was doing more homework, school activities, household work, and over money. It was a heated argument and it was loud, and when it was over, in my head, I was heading for divorce. It was not something I had ever allowed to enter my mind.

The next day, I made sure to leave work at a decent time, get home, fix dinner, and take the kids to practice. By the time he picked them up and got to the dinner table, I remember jokingly engaging the kids in a friendly conversation about which one of their parents they would want to live with if we divorced. Each one chose one of us. Mr. Green Eyes looked me dead in the eyes and told me I could leave whenever I wanted; however, his children were not going anywhere. I laughed at him and told him he was watching too many court TV shows. The reality was I would not have fought him as he was as strong a parent as I, and I'd told him before we were married I would never choose to be a single mother and would gladly pay child support. I'm so grateful we never had to make that choice.

QUESTIONS TO ASK YOURSELF /**for discussion:**

Do you want children?

_____

_____

_____

_____

Have you discussed religion? Up-bringing styles?

_____

_____

_____

_____

Does he believe watching his children is babysitting? You best know the answer to that before pregnancy.

_____

_____

_____

_____

3

GOD IS THE HEAD OF OUR
HOUSEHOLD

I had practiced Catholicism all my life; however, after my son was born, the news of all the sex abuse within the Church began to shake my faith. I spent years searching for a new church home. My search led me to join my husband's family church.

I have a strong faith in God and truly believe there is a Higher Being guiding my life. I also understand my Ancestors and the energy force of those that came before me and stand strong if my faith.

Dating for so long has its advantages. You get to know each other along with their families, circle of friends, and value systems. My father-in-law was a character. Having lost my dad in my 20s, I built quite a relationship with him, and he considered me his daughter long before his son and I married. I shared many wonderful and informative conversations with my Father in Law before we were married.

Since both sets of parents were married in the Catholic Church, neither considered divorce an option. A few months before we were married, my father-in-law mentioned how happy he was that we were getting married in a Catholic Church. He was happy cause Mr. Green Eyes could do what he wanted and I would never leave him. I very sternly said to my father-in-law that, unlike my mother and my future mother-in-law, if my husband did the things that my father and he had done, I would be out of that marriage so damn quickly that the only thing my husband would be able to do was to come home to his parents. I can still see the stunned look on his face. He was not ready for my response, and we never spoke about that again. He became one of our biggest supporters in our marriage and was an excellent grandfather to my children and someone I considered a father and a friend. He gifted us with great memories, stories, and advice.

Once I started going to the AME church, I felt my faith restored and enjoyed going to the "Black church." More and more, Mr. Green Eyes started attending, and it was refreshing to go to church as a family.. After a few years, little by little, Mr. Green Eyes started going to church less often as it was interfering in his Sunday activities. I continued to go without him, often meeting my mother-in-law there, especially if she had babysat the children over the weekend.

One Sunday, someone flirted with me in church. I immediately thought, "Who does that?" I am a married woman in church with my children. I clearly had my wedding band on and was with my mother-in-law. I joked about it with my father-in-law after church. He wasn't much of a churchgoer, but his response left me curious. He simply stated, "Who's the head of your household?"

I very proudly responded, "We are equal partners."

He laughed in my face, a wicked kind of laugh. Then he asked, "Who wears the pants in your household?"

I wasn't so quick to respond this time and asked my mother-in-law the same question. She said something so profound and new to me, it has been a tool ever since. She responded, "God is the head of our household." She shared with me her knowledge of how a strong marriage works, and it was better than what our pre-Cana classes or my parents' marriage had taught me.

The lesson for me from this particular conversation was about beliefs and leadership. I walked away with the following understanding: If you're being led to something and someplace better, you are most likely to follow them. When your husband is a man of God and believes that God is the head of the household, you are more comfortable following your husband, allowing him to lead and represent your household. Being a Christian married to a Christian should not be complicated. There are many biblical stories and accounts of an adult relationship, but not all of them end well. Now do not get it twisted: If Mr. Green Eyes was leading me somewhere crazy, I promise I would not be speaking these words. That is where we need to learn to trust our gut, that sixth sense, your instinct. Do not let a passage from the Bible stop you from following, being led, or loving a good man. Trust your gut.

My mother-in-law and I once discussed keeping your marital business private, and if you had to tell someone, take it to the Lord. She gave pearls of wisdom of staying close, making sure he wanted to come home, keeping your own friends, just a handful. She shared things that touched me in my soul, that fed a part of me that only someone that loved that deeply could share.

Over the years, we would have open and honest conversations, and she fed my soul. My mother-in-law showed me what FAITH looked like, and along with my mother's wisdom on LOVE, I was learning to get out of my own way. I was growing in my faith, my family was thriving, and I was enjoying a successful career.

My daughter's visit to church with her aunt soon found us at a small, non-denominational church, pastored by a man unlike any I had ever witnessed. Watching my Husband grow in his faith and leadership was a real turn on. There is nothing sexier than a man of God; there is an aura that surrounds a man that walks in faith. I was witnessing this growth, and I had never been happier or more in love. This growth period of our marriage formed a bond deeper than I thought possible. I always knew I was deeply in love with my husband, but I actually liked him more now; he was different somehow. We began to call him Deacon Coates, and his smile would appear.

God is the Head of our household. Where He

leads me, I will follow. We believe in something larger than us, and we have built a foundation to fall back on in our spiritually. We pray that our children were paying attention and will find the same love in their lives.

Questions to ask yourself/Discussion:

How will you raise your children? Under whose religion? Are you spiritual?

_____

_____

_____

_____

What feelings does the term "submissive wife" stir in you?

_____

_____

_____

_____

Do you want him to go to your place of worship? Is it non-negotiable?

_____

_____

_____

_____

4

LET'S TALK ABOUT SEX – OOPS GOOD GIRLS DON'T TALK ABOUT SEX; THEY JUST DO IT?

The best part of being the Black girl in a white school was all of the cultural idiosyncrasies I have learned. Masturbation was something boys did. No one in my home girl squad ever mentioned the word without "oh my God I walked in on…" I am not even sure which of my white girls started the conversation, but I was intrigued. Not because it was about sex; they spoke about it in the form of birth control. This hood girl was like what the …? You can touch, feel, and look, and nobody gets pregnant. I was Miss Goody two shoes that I would listen to them tell some guy they had got all worked up that they were saving themselves for the Lord or that they were married to God until he sends her husband. Those were interesting strategies until the high schooler comes up pregnant. Unlike when my mother was in "Catholic school" and was sent to the unwed mother's school, you were allowed to not only go to school pregnant, you were allowed to return post delivery. I always believed the School Administrators thought they would be shamed and shunned. Really, whom were they kidding? We were evolving into a world with less judgment, and sex was leading the way.

My goal was to get out of high school without getting pregnant. We are familiar with "the talk" Black parents have with their children; there is another conversation my mother had with her girls. It was a consistent, Saturday morning house cleaning, on the way up Ritchie Highway conversation. It started with "If you knew what I knew..." fill in the blank. She begged us more than anything to finish high school, not get pregnant while still in school, and to not have babies we couldn't afford. I took her words seriously.

Listening to my mom and dad talk about their relationship after so many years of wonderment, I could not wait to hear their story. I was not horrified by their love story, and my interpretation is a result of asking too many personal questions. My dad was quite the romantic apparently and explained his love for women. My father loved women, and they loved him back. He found it hard to be faithful, and women did not respect his marriage any more than he did. I will not give those women any more of my energy now than I did then. Out of the many that I met to this day, I have respect for one of them, and she and my mom became friends. Let's just say, if someone treated me like I treated them I would have a criminal record. My Granny often used the word debonair to describe my father and once told him to his face, "If you're going to lay with them you should get paid." His response was, "What makes you think I'm not?" Yup, he loved women, and women loved him back.

I wanted the real story, and I will share this: Apparently, my mother enjoyed sex—yup, as a young woman, she enjoyed sex. Daddy often told the story of their practice of the then-popular Catholic birth control "rhythm method." They ended up with six children. His other favorite was that she suffered mood swings when she did not get enough sex. My Sisters and I understood this and often refer to this as suffering from "lackofnooky."

I would ask her about what Daddy said, and she would often have a comeback about not listening or believing everything your Daddy says. Her philosophy with me and my virginity was   "If you don't have it, you won't miss it." Thank God I had older sisters and a brother and had overheard their sex ed conversation with my parents. The lies they tell, talking about "cherry sodas" and "popping cherries." The first conversation she had with me was forced by a pregnancy scare. All these years later, it's the scariest conversation I have ever had in my life. For real for real.

My mom never divorced my dad and spent 40 years with a live-in companion. I came to the realization early that my mom was a woman before she became a mother. I am forever grateful that I learned that lesson early enough in my life to enjoy my relationship with my mother, woman to woman. We spoke about everything. I talked to her like I spoke to my girlfriends, and yes, she finally answered my question. She enjoyed sex and was grateful that her "girls" were not stifled by our Catholic upbringing about sex being for procreation only. She was also grateful that we did not have the need to experiment with many men to find what we wanted. I shared with her that her daughters were moody and evil when suffering from "lackanooky." I was a belly holding laugh fest. The apples did not fall far from her tree.

I tested the theory of celibacy once during a breakup with Mister Green Eyes. I dove back into my religious studies and learned that the marriage vow was made when a woman's hymen was broken, when blood was spilled, and this determined that a woman was considered married to the man that took her virginity. Yeah, that was my thought: Can you imagine being married to the man you lost your virginity to? How many men do you think would marry any of the women with whom they took their virginity? How many women would give their virginity away if they knew they would have to marry that person? This entire thought process kept me celibate.

I read a lot of James 1: 12-16 and 1 Corinthians 10:6-13—praying to overcome temptation—and then I came upon the story of Ruth and Boaz. The Book of Ruth was a game-changer for me. It helped me overcome any Catholic guilt I was feeling for having premarital sex. I am not a prude or judgmental, but I definitely worried about my afterlife and how God would judge me.

If my interpretation about what I read is wrong, God and I will discuss it when I get there. Thinking of sex as pleasing to you and your husband in a seductive setting, to include oral sex, well, that was going in a different direction than anything I learned in religion class, Sunday school, or Bible study. I began to read everything I could about women in the Bible.

For me, celibacy comes from your own personal belief system. You will only be a virgin until you give it away; however, you do not have to have sex if you do not want it. If you desire to wait on a husband to be sexually intimate, marry yourself to God. It's a personal choice, and we should not shame people in their decision.

It's okay to self-pleasure; it's the solution to a lot of our problems, unwanted pregnancy, disease, etc.

QUESTIONS TO ASK YOURSELF/DISCUSSION:

Can you differentiate love from sex? Have you healed your sexual traumas?

_____

_____

_____

_____

Men like to have sex, and so do women. Are you able to ask for what you want in bed?

_____

_____

_____

_____

It's okay to self-pleasure; it's the solution to a lot of our problems, unwanted pregnancy, disease, etc.

_____

_____

_____

_____

5

MIND YOUR MONEY

This is not a chapter on financial planning, although I could certainly write that book; this is about marriage and money.

I grew up poor and did not know it until I was living on my own and making the kind of money as a single woman that my mom made as a single mother of six. How in God's name did she manage that? Her favorite quote was "I'll be robbing Peter to pay Paul this month," but somehow, we all made it through stronger and wiser leaving her house than many of our peers.

I had my first job and bank account at 10 years old. I quickly learned that I could turn my "smartest girl in the neighborhood" into a side hustle. I earned money helping with homework, teaching reading skills, and occasionally just doing the homework so we could all get outside and play.

I became a banker right out of high school in what was supposed to be a summer job. I was learning more about life and survival working with the "Golden Girls." The branch was staffed by all women over 50, married and divorced—boy, do I have stories. I was taking mental notes on a daily basis. These were not the traditional white women that I had been previously exposed to. They were bad-asses, and I am grateful for the lessons they shared and unknowingly taught me. When they spoke about money, it was not the "robbing Peter and paying Paul" conversations; it was about financial plans, secret stashes, and controlling the budgets in their households. They discussed having your own credit, money, bank accounts, and professionals. I listened and learned. These were the conversations I heard when I was at my granny's house. It was making sense to me.

The basic question of "What are you going to do if he leaves?" Now I understood.

When I got married, I knew there were two conversations I had to share with my husband: I was not comfortable with a joint account only and I will always know what it cost to run our household. It was not about secrets, it was about growing up poor, it was about my parents losing it all because Daddy took the insurance money and gambled and the house burnt to the ground, it was about feeding six children on a "new-on-the-job salary."

I often ask my friends how much it costs to run their household. Most do not know, married or single.

I love to entertain, but I am not much of a bar girl, and a lesson learned from watching my granny and listening to her woman friends was about keeping a well-stocked bar. By our third year of marriage, Mr. Green Eyes had several single man friends that were not part of our original circle of friends. They would go out after work and occasionally come to the house. I enjoyed playing hostess and would keep quiet as I got to know them. They would intertwine conversations about their wives and girl-friends. I would listen and take notes.

We received an invitation to a child's birthday party, and I had to tell my husband I was not comfortable taking our child to a birthday party and meeting a wife whose husband cheats on her. He took our son alone.

Once while hosting, one of his friends jokingly (yeah, right) talked about getting Green Eyes a girlfriend. I said without skipping a beat that "if my husband could afford a girlfriend, I'm not spending enough of his money, and let me be certain that you understand that I'm not the forgiving type. The only thing he will be able to afford when I'm done with him is to go home to his mother."

I truly believe it is cheaper to keep her. I am the money manager of our household, and we live a very good life. I don't have any secrets, and I force him to sit through our tax process so he fully understands our cash position.

Mister Green Eyes loves toys and has expensive hobbies. My hobby is investing and traveling. Our children are grown, and we are both looking forward to retiring and traveling, by boat, plane, or motorcycle. We are excited for the next stage.

In the meantime, our bar is at Coates Café. We do happy hour at Coates Café with parties of two or a hundred. It's hard to spend money on a lonely lady at the bar if the bar is in your house. It's hard to blow the rent/mortgage/car payment treating at the bar/lounge/club if your entertainment is budgeted.

Make your home welcoming and happier than Happy Hour, someplace you both enjoy and have fun and save your money. A bar tab can ruin your marriage, break your bank account, and cause legal problems. Flirt with each other at your own bar, in your own house.

We spoke early in our marriage about money, and I voiced often that I didn't want to argue about money. I was honest about everyone in the house having to have a job; I was not taking care of able-bodied adults, and you couldn't come home talking about you been fired over something dumb.

I was also very private about many things in my life then and was certain not to invite people into our marriage that did not play a significant role. People did not have the right to know what was going on in our marriage. It is none of their business, and they should never be comfortable enough to ask personal questions—not our friends and not your in-laws or outlaws.

As we were able to build a lifestyle that was more comfortable than I could have ever imagined, I had to get comfortable discussing our goals with Mr. Green Eyes. The discussion around what was coming in and what was going out. He could care less. As long as there were no past due bills, foreclosures, or the lights were out, he trusted me.

Knowing what our lifestyle cost us has allowed us to live well.

QUESTIONS TO ASK YOURSELF/DISCUSSION:

Are you expecting a man to bring to the table what you cannot?

_____

_____

_____

_____

Have you discussed how you will co-mingle your money?

_____

_____

_____

_____

Have you asked for or been asked to sign a prenup? Would you?

_____

_____

_____

_____

6

50/50 IS A LIE

I remember calling my sister and complaining about how I was not feeling supported. That I was doing more than my share and literally bitching and throwing divorce all in the atmosphere. She very calmly said to me, "Who told you that marriage was 50/50?"

I was like, "What? What are you talking about?"

We proceeded to have a long conversation about what a partnership really was. She explained that a real partnership requires the partner to carry the load at different times. Sometimes it's 50/50, sometimes it's 99/1, and sometimes you carry the whole 100 percent. She shared some things about her own marriage that I only knew half the story. That weekend we got together, and she truly enlightened me about a real marriage built on love, trust, and sacrifice.

It was a lesson of love, laughter, and learning. I love my sister deeply, and her raw honestly taught me a very valuable lesson. It helped me view her marriage with respect and honor and gave me permission to proceed with a different mindset in my own marriage.

Developing a partnership within a marriage is not as easy as it seems. Someone is always feeling they are doing more than the other. For me, it required an end game—What will happen if I support this unconditionally? What will happen if I make the sacrifice? How will he respond if I ask for something that men do not traditionally do? What will happen if I trust him completely?

I took my sister's advice. She had been through some things, and I trusted her. She had never led me wrong.

I began to ask for what I needed to get us to the end game. Mr. Green Eyes once went on the night shift, and we determined he would be in charge of taking the kids to daytime appointments. This worked very well the first year or so. Then it started interfering in his motorcycle rides and weekend fun. Suddenly it was my fault that I scheduled these appointments at these times and we were spending time at sporting events and team practices. I had to gently remind him that it was in "our" best interest that he took this shift, that we were saving money by not having daycare, aftercare, etc.

I wasn't being selfish; I was holding up my end of the deal. I was sacrificing you not being home with us overnight. This was not about making it easier to ride your motorcycle or hangout with your friends. You have to choose sleep over riding.

What is your end game? It required me to leave work at a decent time, have dinner with my family, and get it done so he could get his sleep and go to work. It was a sacrifice for both of us that played well for our end game. Our kids got through school, doctor, and dental appointments and were able to participate in sports and other social activities and have their parents participate and offer guidance.

Not everything is equal, and what works for one couple will not work for every couple. Define your needs, ask for what you need, and be willing to make sacrifices. Sometimes you will have to carry the full load, and sometimes you have to give your partner the full load. If you are in this together, you will win together.

QUESTIONS TO ASK YOURSELF/DISCUSSION:

How are your negotiation skills?

_____
_____
_____
_____

What do your marital duties look like? Do you feel they are fair?

_____
_____
_____
_____

Are you prepared to carry the marriage 100 percent of the time?

_____
_____
_____
_____

7

TRUST: NON NEGOTIABLES=JOBS, OUTSIDE CHILDREN AND AFFORDING GIRLFRIENDS

*W*hen I realized I was in love, it struck me like a ton of bricks. I was a collector of boyfriends and a serial dater at a very young age. I was also a proud virgin—you could look, feel, and touch, but I was not peanut butter, and you were not going to spread me around.

I had watched my parents' relationship, and I observed the things that made my mom the saddest. I watched her mannerism and expressions and listened to her words when she spoke of these things. Even now, years later, these things haunt me as non-negotiables that would end my marriage. There were two—yes, only two things that I knew would end my marriage.

1. I got fired and have to find another job because of something dumb.

2. I have a baby coming.

The only way two of us not getting up and going to work is if you are physically not able to get up and go. I am not living with anyone and his or her fake disability that limits income. Lazy is just not sexy, and fast money scares me. What type of man doesn't want his own money? A boy-man, that's who. I'm not into boys; I require a full-grown man. A man who could survive without me, not quickly moving to the next woman to have somewhere to live, put money in his pocket, and make sure he has a nice ride.

Grown-ass men are sexy as fuck, and those with a paycheck carry themselves differently. Grown-ass women do not mind having the backs of grown-ass men.

If you have been fired for some asinine reason, such as struggling while Black, I get that, but you best pick up some applications on the way home and get some references on the way out the door.

I know many Women raising their Sons to be dependent on them. That is not a good look for your sons and it surely does not prepare them to leave home. What do you think happens to a grown man with no job prospects, history and who has never had to be responsible for anything? He is on your cuch, living in your house forever. These mothers consistently side with their sons, whether they are right or wrong. These are not men raised to own their Ish and they are not ready for a grown woman. They are not the Marrying Type because they are their mothers Boyfriends, yup I said it. They treat their Boys like their boyfriends and take issue with the Women that fall in love with them and call them out.

I grew up in a household where my father had outside children, and this was a huge non-negotiable for me. Every breakup Mr. Green Eyes and I had, I would tell him the same thing. "You cannot come back to me with a child." It was something my 10-year-old self carried into adulthood. I watched my family fall apart when my dad showed up with his girlfriend and their baby at my momma's house, his wife's house. I still feel the rage of his selfishness, having the audacity to think his behavior was okay. This was not a respectful example for his three sons, my brothers, my sisters or me.

The feeling of fathering children without responsibility, discounting their mother and moving on to the next mother left me bitter toward my father. It left me very uncomfortable to date men with children. I could not do it. Listening to men badmouth the mother of their children, the name-calling of money-hungry ... I once asked a date how much he paid in child support, and it barely covered meals for a month. Some men are just clueless, actually saying they babysit their children—no, fool, you're watching them like we do most of the time. I was not stepmother material.

Since he grew up under the same circumstances and knew his own mother's pain, he understood. In the '80s when we were dating, I also found it irresponsible that men were having multiple sex partners and not using condoms. This said to me that not only were you sleeping around fathering kids, you are having unprotected sex. This was the largest statement of how disrespectful you were to me. You would be willing to jeopardize my health, and I now have to live with this forever. No, thanks.

Having to deal with another woman with a say in my marriage, dictating money, vacations, when, where, and how's in my space and a husband in her space, even if they don't interact in the child's day-to-day life, your life is affected—I opted out of this life.

How does this affect your children? It is all about

trust. They now know Daddy is unfaithful, how can we trust him? Daddy issues are real and way above my paygrade to evaluate and speak on. I only know what I've lived through and witnessed with my siblings and observed in my circle. You live in towns and stare at children that look like you and your siblings, how do you not feel the impact? You then look back at your momma and feel her pain and see her struggle and understand why she left.

How do you trust? Nope, non-negotiable for me.

QUESTIONS TO ASK YOURSELF/DISCUSSION:

How does your family dynamic allow you to trust or not to trust? Did your parents discuss trust with each other or as a family?

_____
_____
_____
_____

Is there a legacy of distrust in your relationship? How do you think marriage will change that?

_____
_____
_____
_____

Are there others involved in your relationships that have nothing to add? Who invited them into the relationship?

_____
_____
_____
_____

8

GETTING OUT OF YOUR HEAD

*W*e have all created scenarios that do not really exist, things that have not actually happened, and visuals of imaginative scenes of you catching your mate out with someone else. Role-playing in your head the reason why they're late to get home, why they have not returned your text. Who is he really hanging out with when the fellas are stopping to get a drink after work?

Whew, the energy I have wasted on those scenes in my head.

I have always been a social butterfly. Mr. Green Eyes and I were and are a scenario of opposites attracting and were in love when we married.

When the kids came, they were the priority:

School, sports, their social life, meeting parents, etc., etc. became my social playground. If he volunteered, it was a rarity. It became the new normal. My kids were happy and thriving, and I stayed busy with work and their social lives.

As they became more independent, I began to make more time for my friends, even making new friends, which had never been easy for me. I found it interesting that he never questioned where I was going or who I was with. If he asked, I was always honest, responded to texts, and picked up if he called. He knew my truth, and he trusted me. He wasn't drumming up some scenario of me laying up with someone else.

So why was I? Trust. He trusted me.

Why was I allowing my own insecurity to fester and cause me to mistrust my husband, who had not given me one reason not to trust him? It was something I had to work through, and I really did not know where to start. Meditation helped, and getting out of my own head helped. Rewriting the scene playing in my head helped.

After one particular night, I blew up and told him how disrespected I felt that he didn't feel the need to touch base when he wasn't going to be home when he said he was, especially if he was out on his motorcycle, and the lying on the road scene that played in my head.

He reminded me that we had worked hard to obtain the love and trust we had in our lives, and we both had too much to lose to allow someone else to benefit from the work we had put into this relationship.

I had to explain to him that sometimes I did not feel heard, or that he was discounting my opinion, which closed off my heart. He would voice his opinion and his needs as if I was supposed to automatically agree with him and forget my own needs. I would get all in my head because I would not give in to him.

This became a game of ego for me. I always had his back, and I needed him to reassure me that he had mine.

Do not get me wrong: If it is not working for you, and your gut is telling you something is not right, that is different. Remember if it is worth fighting for, then you should fight. Let go of the demons in your head.

The recent events have shined a light on mental

health. There is no shame or judgment to seek help to understand the "why" of your life. Use your EAP from work for therapy, counseling, pastoral, and even couple therapy/counseling.

QUESTIONS TO ASK YOURSELF/DISCUSSION

Do you trust your partner? Is there a reason not to trust your partner?

_____

_____

_____

_____

Do you feel heard in the relationship? Do you discuss your feelings?

_____

_____

_____

_____

Pre-marriage counseling is recommended: does your church/temple offer? Are you open to seeing a marriage counselor, therapist, speaking with a third party?

_____

9

DATE NIGHT AND BIBLE STUDY

hen we finally found a church home that we were both comfortable with, we began to go to Bible study. This was new for us and was strengthening our marriage and our family bond.

During one particular study, we got on the discussion of the "submissive wife." The women were shocked to hear me say that I considered myself a submissive wife. Not me the successful banker, mother, sister girl; yes, me. It goes right back to who is leading your household. It was such a hot topic that night that we went out to dinner to continue the discussion.

It eventually became date night. We would leave Bible study and go to dinner. The kids were older and had their own lives; however, they would occasionally join us, and we would have deep conversations about family and church. We expanded date night to include weekend time with just the two of us. As fans of live music, we sought out good music, delicious food, and fun. We were enjoying each other as individuals, not just parents.

It gave us time to catch up and stay in tune with each other. Even with adult children, we knew we had to stay connected.

One night we were out really enjoying the evening, I found myself on the phone texting someone and on Facebook, totally distracted. I got a text. It was from Mr. Green Eyes, reminding me that we were on a date. I found it cute but a real reminder on the purpose of our date nights was for us to reconnect. I began to keep my phone in my purse.

During this time, our friends were beginning to get divorced, and we were becoming more aware of what could happen if we did not continue to communicate and voice our needs as individuals and as a couple unit. We also began to realize we craved activities that the others had no interest in. We have gotten more comfortable over the years, that this is okay. We have to be okay with having separate interests and not feel that we are being selfish to take time to do things that we like to do and respect each other's time and commitment to those things.

This process has been elevated because we have learned to communicate with each other and make the time we spend together more important and more of a priority.

I am grateful that we had a church family that mirrored this and allowed us to express ourselves while learning to build a family unit and a strong foundation for our children. This was one of the happiest times of my life.

QUESTIONS TO ASK YOURSELF/DISCUSSION:

Are you still dating your spouse? Are you connected?

_____

_____

_____

_____

Where does your belief system fit in your relationship? Have you tested your spiritual realm?

_____

_____

_____

_____

Change it up—you should both be enjoying date night.

_____

_____

_____

_____

10

SHOWING UP FOR EACH OTHER

*L*et's be real. Marriage is hard work, very hard, and not everyone is cut out to put in the work required to make it last.

As individuals, everyone's star rises differently. I've been blessed that my star has always been bright and has shined most of my life, with occasional dims. I'm not shy about asking for help or telling people what I need. It's a blessing and a curse.

It took many years of marriage temper tantrums, not speaking for days around the house, and questioning my sanity and his intellect to realize sometimes he just won't show up for me. It hurts.

It's a selfish decision that leads to the same conversation and argument. He's selfish and didn't think he'd done anything wrong.

I've had a number of significant recognitions in my career that he has not shown up, and I watched for years as he showed up for others. In one month, he missed our family vacation, graduation, and my birthday, and never apologized.

I could set the calendar around Mother's Day, birthdays and Christmas. I have no scientific evidence; however, I'm convinced it's a holdover from their single days when they didn't want to buy a woman a gift. He became really good at ruining Christmas, which by the way he is a holiday baby. I was determined he would not ruin Christmas for the kids. I have always tried to celebrate his birthday separate from Christmas. This takes a lot of time, effort, and planning. I always wanted him to feel special for his birthday before jumping into Christmas.

He got the kids excited about the tree farm, the largest tree we could cut ourselves. He would set the tree up, and then he was done.

I would do all the planning, shopping, and coordinating menus, cleaning, cooking, wrapping, and decorating, and he would watch. One year he got on his motorcycle and went for a ride. Yup, in December. I was livid and knew that would be the last year I would go over the top. I was done.

That year I learned to protect my peace. I learned to be okay with myself. I knew how it would play out, the excuses he would make, and that he didn't know I needed him to do anything. After all of these years, he knew exactly what went into gathering two families for a holiday dinner, and I was tired. This year I was dealing with knowing that it would be my Mother's last Christmas with me. I was an emotional mess, and he didn't show up for me. It hurt.

I have tended to my husband through major surgeries, and for him to behave as if he could not reciprocate and support me was hurtful and selfish.

I learned then what my mother meant when she said, "Sometimes you have to show them better than you can tell them and show up for yourself."

It was during this time that my cheerleading squad showed up. They supported me. Everyone needs a squad who you can trust—the good, the bad, and the ugly. Your marriage cannot survive without them. Just as important is to be part of someone else's squad.

Two-sided relationships are very important, and you cannot, will not, and should not expect one person to be all of that for you.

I have the expectation that my husband will give me the love and support I need. I am also mature enough to ask for what I need and more importantly, to hold him accountable when I don't get it and then move the fuck on. Knowing that if I am stuck in that funk... Well, Houston, we have a problem.

I have learned for me that when I fester in this place, my behavior changes, and I want everyone who has not met my expectation to pay the price. In reality, he has already moved on to the next thing, and I am still fuming.

I've learned how easy it is for him to say no to me and began to take lessons out of his playbook and say no to him for things I really didn't want to do but was willing because he asked. "No, I don't want to do that" became easier.

When he questions why, I very calmly say—and I mean calmly—"When I asked you to do ... you said no, and I felt unsupported, and right now I can't support you for something I really don't want to do." The more you say no, the more they pay attention. This is not the time to let your insecurities creep in.

Let them show up alone a few times and people start asking questions, remind them without reminding them what you bring to the table. Show up for yourself—put yourself first. You deserve it.

I don't consider myself needy; however, this is a

partnership, and give and take go both ways. I truly love my husband; however, this lesson taught me that I needed to love myself more, I needed to speak up for myself louder, and I needed to be selfish sometimes for me. Self-care is me putting my oxygen mask on first. I'm much better at this now than I've ever been, and I'm happier.

One of my best friends told me to get on top of the mountain of my life and look down; What do you see? I have a good life and much to be proud of. We have learned from this difficult time and are stronger because of what we have weathered together.

We communicate our pain points and support each other through our individual needs. We don't try to be the end-all for each other but are there to support each other.

QUESTIONS TO ASK YOURSELF/DISCUSSION:

Do you have a lifeline of trustworthy friends outside of your marriage?

Do you feel heard in your marriage? Do you have a listening ear?

Are you able to ask for what you need? Even when it's hard?

11

THINK ABOUT IT

For those who have been married for more than five years, sit around with each other and consider the following questions to move you to the next five years.

Who won your last argument/disagreement? What was it about? What part of it are you still holding on to?

How much does it cost to run your household? How often do you argue/disagree about money?

How often do you have sex? Who initiates? Do you enjoy it?

Do not let others define you or your marriage. Whom should you evict from your marriage?

Are you kind to each other?

Do you have an open mind?

Stay focused—two positives to one negative. Say something nice.

Visualize your future. What does it look like? Are you preparing for it? Do you check in to see that you are still on the same page?

Learn something new. One thing you each want to try. Try it together.

Stay true to your values.

LAUGH EVERY DAY.

12
KNOW THY SELF

*a*s I approached my most significant career opportunity, I became scared, unsure of what it would look like and what it would do to my home life. It was a huge promotion.

I knew that I wanted it and truly felt like what benefited me benefited us. My former First Lady of the Church would always say "the one of us," and I adopted that mentality when it came to my relationship and marriage.

This promotion elevated our lifestyle to ensure we would be able to support our children in their next phase of life as well as afford us to have some fun and travel. For me, it gave me the focus I needed to plan for the retirement I totally intend to enjoy.

I know what I know, and I love whom I love. I

did not intend to let a generous salary destroy or come between what we'd built. However, I did feel the need to discuss it with Mr. Green Eyes. Not all men are comfortable when their spouse's salary exceeds theirs.

My Grand Pop had taught me that a man needs to feel needed and to never say to a man that you don't need him. He taught me to make moves to please myself, to take care of myself, and once he saw what you bring to the table, a real man will not want another man at the table with you.

The truth of the matter is my relationship is all about loyalty. I will always be loyal to those who are loyal to me. I'm not sharing my man; we're either all in, or I'm out. You can't be married acting single.

Talk about maturity. We had come a long way from some of his archaic ideas of marriage. He had matured and understood this was not about me, but us. He understood that if I was good, we were good. I also knew that he was not going anywhere, and he teased that if I wanted to leave, I could as long as I left the paycheck and that I could not take the kids. It was a running joke that he needed alimony, child support, and the mortgage paid. We were on solid ground.

I have continued to pursue a promising career

that I love, have obtained a senior vice president title which I never thought I would hold, have supported many not-for-profits in director roles, and I'm excited about my future.

He supports my dreams, and we recognize that our joint happiness prospers.

We will celebrate our 30th wedding anniversary in 2021. We survived the COVID pandemic, the death of my loving mother, and two major surgeries. We are still standing and putting in the work necessary to get to our 50th anniversary.

I truly cannot imagine my life without Mr. Green Eyes and all of the love and privilege that we enjoy as a "Black love" couple. We have a strong village of people that love us, pray for us, and cheer us on. They also call us out when needed and keep us accountable to each other.

I am the marrying type, and I'm blessed that I married my best friend and soul mate, who is also the marrying type.

Thirty years and counting. We reached our Sturdy 30, and I can't wait for our Nifty 50.

Are you the marrying type?

ABOUT THE AUTHOR

Michelle Johnson Coates grew up in a low-income neighborhood in Eastport, Maryland. She realized her life could go one of two ways, so she created her own luck.

Mrs. Coates fell in love and married her high school sweetheart, Kenny Coates. Together, they are enjoying the ride on the motorcycle or being lazy out on the boat; they are living their best lives.

She is a dedicated mother of two amazing adult children: Kenny, Jr. a boatswain mate in the United

States Coast Guard, and Kelsey, an environmental scientist at John Hopkins University.

Michelle has made a difference in the lives of young girls in that same neighborhood, knowing firsthand the impact that a mentor can make on a young girl or teen's life.

Michelle is a believer that you should give your time, talent, or treasure and has previously volunteered with the Annapolis-based non-profit, Seeds 4 Success, as a mentor for the Eastport Girls Club program. Michelle continues to support the program financially, as a sponsor of their signature "Cocktails for a Cause" event.

As a former board member of the Anne Arundel County Public Library Foundation, Michelle completed an extended tenure as the treasurer, helping to guide the team to a successful campaign to raise over $1M.

She is currently the vice chair for the Maryland Council of Economic Education Association. As a seasoned banker, she is excited to share her experiences with the educators/teachers and students to better prepare them for the future. Michelle is looking forward to advocating for financial literacy in our school systems throughout the State of Maryland and more specifically in Anne Arundel County.

Michelle surrounds herself with a strong village of women warriors that keep her lifted in prayer, supplied with wine, and laughing uncontrollably at Mr. Green Eyes and his antics.

Made in the USA
Middletown, DE
11 August 2022

71131368R00044